GRANT HILL

GRANT HILL
HUMBLE HOTSHOT

Jeff Savage

 Lerner Publications Company • Minneapolis

To my dad

Information for this book was obtained from the following sources:
Basketball America, Beckett Basketball, Change The Game by Grant Hill, *The Dallas Morning News, Detroit Free Press, The Detroit News, Durham Herald-Sun, Esquire, Gentleman's Quarterly, The New York Times, Oakland Press, People, Philadelphia Daily News, St. Petersburg Times, Sidekicks International, Sports Illustrated, The Sporting News, USA Today, The Washington Post.*

This book is available in two editions:
Library binding by Lerner Publications Company
Soft cover by First Avenue Editions
241 First Avenue North, Minneapolis, Minnesota 55401
International Standard Book Number: 0-8225-2893-2 (lib. bdg.)
International Standard Book Number: 0-8225-9751-9 (pbk.)

LIBRARY OF CONGRESS CATALOGING-IN-PUBLICATION DATA

Savage, Jeff.
    Grant Hill : humble hotshot / Jeff Savage.
        p.   cm.
    Summary: A biography of the Duke University basketball star who went on to become co-Rookie of the Year with the Detroit pistons in the 1994–95 season.
    ISBN 0-8225-2893-2 (hardcover : alk. paper).
    ISBN 0-8225-9751-9 (pbk. : alk. paper)
    1. Hill, Grant—Juvenile literature.   2. Basketball players—United States—Biography—Juvenile literature. [1. Hill, Grant. 2. Basketball players. 3. Afro-Americans—Biography.]   I. Title.
GV884.H55S28   1997
796.323'092—dc20
[B]   96–25067

Manufactured in the United States of America
1 2 3 4 5 6 – JR – 02 01 00 99 98 97

Contents

The Fans' Favorite

Grant Hill suddenly realized his situation. He was standing between Shaquille O'Neal and Scottie Pippen, in front of 20,000 people at the America West Arena in Phoenix, Arizona. They were about to be introduced for the 1995 National Basketball Association All-Star Game. Grant was just a rookie. He had played with the Detroit Pistons only three months. He was so embarrassed to be standing with the basketball superstars that he wished he could vanish from sight.

But it isn't easy for Grant Hill to hide. After all, he's 6 feet 8 inches tall, with a head shaped like a lightbulb. His body is thin and angular, except for his shoulders, which are wide. His eyes are soft and round and curious, and his ears stick out from his shaved head like a pair of bat wings. "He has the most perfect body I've ever seen," says one coach. "He's perfectly proportioned, and it makes him the most deceiving player in the world."

Grant has what is called a complete game. He can rebound, pass, dribble, play defense, shoot from the outside, and fly to the basket for acrobatic dunks. He has no weakness. And, like Michael Jordan, Grant performs most of his magic in the air.

But an All-Star as a rookie? One of the 12 best players in the NBA's Eastern Conference? Grant couldn't believe it. "I don't think I deserve to be on the team," he said. But fans across the country thought he did. Each year, the fans vote on which players should be in the starting lineups. The fans had voted for Grant to be a starter. Grant got more votes than any other player! More than Hakeem Olajuwon, more than Charles Barkley, more than everyone else. A rookie never did that before. Not even the great Jordan.

How did Grant Hill become so popular so fast? In a sport with much taunting and trash-talking, Grant is a breath of fresh air. He doesn't draw attention to himself with jewelry or dyed hair or loud-mouthing or flashy dances. "Don't get me wrong—I talk on the court," Grant says. "When a guy makes a nice move, I tell him 'Nice move.'"

Grant carries himself with grace and dignity. He is genuine and humble. Fans love him for it. So do companies. Before his first professional season even started, Grant had been hired by several major corporations to represent their products.

Grant is a talented musician who enjoys playing the piano, especially for young fans.

He was making a commercial for Wilson Sporting Goods Company the day he heard about the All-Star voting. "Smile," photographers told him as he posed with a basketball in one hand and a textbook in the other. "Now, look serious," they instructed him as their cameras clicked away. During a break in the filming, Grant was told of being the NBA's leading vote-getter. "Impossible," he said.

A week later in Phoenix, a blue spotlight from high in the arena rafters streamed down on Grant as his name was announced. He blushed and jogged out to center court. "I just didn't want to trip," he said. His parents, Calvin and Janet, stood in the crowd and applauded. Calvin had been a star running back for the Dallas Cowboys, Washington Redskins, and Cleveland Browns. Janet is vice president of a company and was a Wellesley College roommate of Hillary Rodham Clinton, President Clinton's wife.

Grant was so jittery he felt his knees shaking. Fireworks exploded overhead and he nearly collapsed from fright. "I thought somebody was trying to shoot me," he said.

The game began with Grant playing in the small forward spot. He wears jersey No. 33 for the Pistons, but for this game he wore No. 35 in honor of his father. Calvin Hill wore No. 35 while leading the Cowboys to their first Super Bowl.

The second time the Eastern Conference team had the ball, guard Anfernee "Penny" Hardaway saw Grant streaking up the baseline. Hardaway threw an alley-oop pass toward the hoop. Grant caught it with both hands, pumped once as he soared over Shawn

Kemp, and slammed it home for a rim-rattling dunk. The crowd went berserk. Grant didn't. "When I make a basket I don't pump my fist," he said. "I turn it into positive energy on the defensive end." Calvin Hill never spiked the football after a touchdown either.

Later in the first quarter, Grant took a pass from Reggie Miller, rose up over Latrell Sprewell, and hit a 10-foot jump shot. He also added three assists and two steals before taking a seat on the bench.

The Eastern Conference trailed by eight points late in the half when Grant returned to give his team a lift. "Be ready, G," Joe Dumars told the nervous rookie. "The ball's coming your way." Joe and Grant are teammates in Detroit and good friends. They play well together with the Pistons, and they teamed up on three straight plays in this game. First Joe bounced a pass inside to Grant, who posted up on Charles Barkley. Grant spun past Barkley as quick as light through a window. Seven-footer Dikembe Mutombo blocked Grant's path to the basket, so Grant lofted a soft floater over Mutombo's long arm. The shot went in. On the next play, Joe threw an alley-oop pass that Grant caught in midair. He cradled the ball with one hand as he glided to the basket and then slammed it down with a tomahawk jam. Finally Joe found Grant breaking free of his defender along the baseline. Grant made the jump shot, giving him 10 points in the first half.

David Robinson, left, and Shawn Kemp try to stop Grant from scoring during the 1995 All-Star Game.

Grant's performance did not calm him. In the locker room at halftime he looked around and thought, "Oh my God! Look at all these great players. What am I doing here?" He became so nervous he nearly got sick to his stomach. Feeling queasy, he played only a few minutes in the second half and did not score again. The Eastern Conference lost, 139–112.

Afterward, Grant was still excited. "When I get back home," he told reporters, "I'm going to call my friends up and say, 'I was in a room with Patrick Ewing!' Or, 'I was in a room with David Robinson!' It was just amazing. I am so lucky."

Before he could go home though, Grant was on his way to more adventures. Right after the game, he boarded a plane and flew off to New York City where he would appear on ESPN's Espy Awards show and then be the featured guest and play the piano on *The Late Show with David Letterman.* The next morning he would fly back to Detroit for a game that night against the Knicks.

"This is all new to me," Grant said about his whirl-wind life as America's new favorite player. "It's exciting and I love it. But it gets me so exhausted. Sometimes I wish I could just be a rookie, learning as I go, instead of whatever this is."

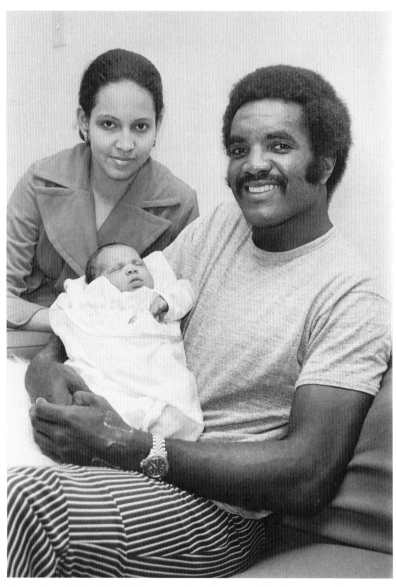

Janet and Calvin Hill proudly show off their son, Grant.

A Sport of His Own

Calvin and Janet Hill met at a party after a college football game. Calvin was the star running back for Yale University, and he had scored every one of his team's touchdowns during its 29–29 tie with Harvard University. He had played the game with stitches in his tongue, which he had split open in a game the previous week. He was only able to mumble, but at the party he managed to ask Janet to dance. She said yes. Two years later, after Janet completed her master's degree in mathematics and education at the University of Chicago, they were married. Calvin was playing for the Cowboys then, and they made their home in Dallas. Two years later, on October 5, 1972, Grant was born. He would be their only child.

For the first three days of his life, Grant was known simply as "Baby Boy Hill." Calvin had wanted a boy. He had wanted a boy so much that he only thought of girls' names so he wouldn't jinx himself. Calvin and Janet came up with different names to give to their new son but they couldn't choose one. Finally Roger Staubach, the Cowboys quarterback, grew tired of their indecision and said, "That's it. It's time to name him, and we're going to name him Grant."

Grant's body grew so quickly that for the first two years of his life he had to wear leg braces in bed to keep from becoming bowlegged. The doctor wanted to break both of Grant's legs to straighten them but Grant's parents said no. Grant is still slightly bowlegged.

When Grant was three, Calvin was traded to the Washington Redskins. The Hill family moved to Reston, Virginia, an upper middle-class suburb near Washington, D.C. The Hills lived on a little street with 12 houses and kids in every house. Grant walked with his friends every day through the woods behind his house to Terraset Elementary School.

Grant's athletic career began when he was five. He joined the Reston Flying Tigers soccer team. He played left-side forward. When he was 10, the Flying Tigers won the Virginia youth league state title. "Being able to tell all my friends that we were state champions was quite a moment for a 10-year-old kid," he says. The Flying Tigers won the title again when he was 12. He stopped playing soccer a year later to concentrate on basketball.

Grant started playing basketball when he was seven.

Janet and Grant, who was 15 months old when this photograph was taken, kept Calvin company while he was recovering from a dislocated elbow.

His mother took him to Tuesday and Friday night games at nearby South Lakes High School.

He joined a club team a year later but didn't have much fun at first. He was the team's tallest player so the coach made him stand under the basket. He rarely touched the ball. One day Grant's dad told him to take the inbounds pass and dribble the ball up-court. The coach saw that Grant could dribble as well as anybody. From then on, Grant dribbled the ball up the court for his team.

Grant didn't play basketball with his junior high team. He didn't do anything else either. He was afraid his schoolmates would like him only because he had a famous father. He imagined their whispers. "Here comes the rich kid," he imagined them saying. "Here comes Calvin Hill's boy." So he took no chances. He avoided everyone. He made no close friends. He was too shy. He came straight home every day and played soccer on the street with the neighborhood fifth-graders.

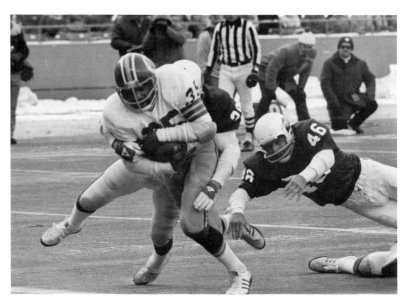

While playing running back, Calvin scores a touchdown for the Washington Redskins.

When Grant was 13, he played for a local team in an Amateur Athletic Union tournament. Grant was 6-foot-3, so he played center. In the championship game, Grant's club played a powerful team from Detroit. Chris Webber and Jalen Rose, two future NBA stars, played for the Detroit team. Grant played a great game and led his team to an upset victory.

Grant's father saw the game and knew Grant was filled with confidence. He decided to test his son when they got home. Calvin was an inch taller than Grant. He had wrestled with Grant on the living room floor and boxed with him in the kitchen doorway.

"So you think you can beat your old man now, huh Grant?" he said. Grant looked at him. "Yeah," he said. They played one-on-one in the driveway basketball court, two games to 11 points. Grant won both easily. "I was shocked he was physically able to beat me," Calvin recalls. Grant rolls his eyes when he hears his dad say that. "He was just another chump to me," Grant says laughing.

Calvin never talked to Grant about working hard. Calvin just worked hard and Grant watched. Calvin would take Grant to the park every day to watch him get in shape for another year with the Redskins. Running. Jumping. Lifting. Stretching. Straining. "He'd never let up," says Grant. "He'd work and he'd sweat and he never stopped. I know now what he was trying to show me. He was showing me that you had to work all the time, on or off the field, in or out of the classroom. Work. Work. Work. He was telling me that was the answer."

Grant's mother ran a Capitol Hill consulting firm and his father played professional football. Not surprisingly, their house was always filled with politicians and sports stars. Grant grew up listening to quarterback Billy Kilmer, tight end Ozzie Newsome, running back John Riggins, receivers Paul Warfield and Art Monk, Senator Bill Bradley, and White House advisor Clifford Alexander. "It was almost like being born into a royal family," Grant says, "and being raised like a prince, being taught one day to become king."

Alexander, for instance, taught Grant the importance of writing. Alexander made Grant write him one letter each week. "I see now what he was doing," Grant says. "He was teaching me, one, discipline. I had to send that letter every week. And, two, he was showing me how to think. He taught me to write and now I like to write. It's a great way of communicating."

Grant worked for Senator Bradley in Washington during the summer between his junior and senior years in high school. He worked in the senator's mail room. "Bill would talk to me about being a success in life," Grant remembers. "He'd tell me about politics, how it worked and how it was a worthy pursuit because you could help other people. He'd tell me that one day I could be a politician and help others."

Janet Hill runs a consulting firm in Washington, D.C.

Grant also admired tennis player Arthur Ashe and basketball star Julius Erving. But he was especially fortunate to have parents who were guiding lights. "I didn't have to look for role models," he says. "They were right down the hall."

As proud as he was of his parents, he was also embarrassed by them. In eighth grade, when his father agreed to speak at Grant's school, Grant pretended he was sick. He hid in the nurse's office. Once when his father met him after basketball practice in his Porsche, Grant asked him to drive the family's Volkswagen next time. "I just wanted to blend in and be like everybody else," said Grant. "I didn't want anybody to think I was better than them."

That became a problem in basketball. Grant was better than anybody else. His father had one sports rule: No football until high school. By the time Grant reached high school, he had lost interest in football. He only wanted to play basketball.

Grant was called into the South Lakes High School coaches' office one day. He had just turned 14. He was a freshman. Basketball coach Wendell Byrd had seen Grant play on the AAU club the year before. Coach Byrd told Grant he was good enough to play for the varsity. Grant had spent the previous season behind the South Lakes bench, passing out water to the players and eating Starbursts. Now he would get to play on the team. It was a great opportunity. But Grant hung his head and said no. Coach Byrd thought he heard wrong. "Now, just wait a second," he said. The coach went through a list of varsity candidates. He would say a name, then ask, "Are you better than him?" Each time, after an embarrassed pause, Grant would say yes. But he still said no to playing varsity. Coach Byrd told him to go home and talk it over with his parents. Then the coach called them.

When Grant got home he didn't mention anything. Finally his father asked him about it. Grant became very upset. "Grant," his father said, "this is a wonderful opportunity." Grant started crying. His parents pleaded with him to explain what the matter was but he wouldn't. "Well," Grant finally said, sniffling, "if you guys make me do it, that's child abuse, making me do something I don't want to do."

Everything was fine the next day. Grant talked it over with his friends. They were all for him playing varsity. He deserved it, they told him. He joined the varsity that afternoon. "I just didn't want to jump ahead of my friends," Grant explained. "I didn't want them thinking that I was better than them." Grant scored an average of 14 points a game that first year. Toward the end of the season, he got his first recruiting letter from a college. Denny Crum, the coach of the University of Louisville, sent it.

Grant watched hours of basketball every night. He taped NBA games that were shown on TV. He went to many Georgetown University Hoyas games and recorded them with his camcorder. He studied plays over and over, memorized moves, ran the tapes in slow motion, rewound them, and ran them again. In two years he broke five remote controls.

Grant would practice moves in his driveway. "I couldn't wait to re-create from memory a move I just saw," he said. When it was too late to be outside, Grant would sneak into the basement and toss the ball off the wall at an imaginary basket. Sometimes he would get into trouble for that. Sometimes his parents would leave him alone.

By his sophomore season, Grant was 6-foot-6 and he could dunk. He averaged 25 points a game and was named Northern Virginia Player of the Year. His average dropped to 17 points a game his junior year—"for the good of the team," he said—but he was Player of the Year again as he led his team to the state finals. All of it wasn't good enough for his father, however, who was hard on Grant.

During Grant's senior year at South Lakes High School, he kept up his grades while averaging 30 points a game for the basketball team.

At home, after every game, Grant had to face what he and his mother called the PGA, the postgame analysis. Calvin would pick apart Grant's game. Calvin would tell him that he had to go more to his left hand, that he had to look to score more, that he had to be more intense on defense. When Grant would say, "I know that," his father would respond, "Oh, so now I have a son who knows everything." Grant learned to keep quiet.

"I'd listen even though I didn't want to," he said. "I tried to just blow it off afterward. I mean, the thing is, my father doesn't know a thing about basketball. He's got that football mentality. It's just his athletic ego. But in a way I'm lucky. It would've been 10 times worse if I played football."

Calvin was so intense that Grant would sometimes defy him by pretending he didn't care about an upcoming game. Calvin had a pregame routine so Grant made a point to not have one.

Before a game, Grant would play or juggle a soccer ball around the house. His father would ask, "Aren't you going to lie down, put your feet up?" Grant would sometimes leave the house little more than an hour before game time. He would putter around the house just to annoy his dad.

"Where's the preparation?" Calvin would say. "You've got to get mentally focused." Grant would leave the house giggling.

Grant's mother was loving but also very strict. Grant's friends nicknamed her "The Sergeant." Grant demanded a higher rank. She became known around the neighborhood as "The General."

Grant was not allowed to make any phone calls during the week. He was permitted a single call on the weekend, but only one and it had a 30-minute limit. There were no parties, no dances, and his TV viewing was limited. He had to be in the house at a certain time, and there was absolutely no leaving the neighborhood.

"They were too strict, if you ask me," he said. "I didn't make any mistakes as a kid because I couldn't. They mapped out my whole life for me to the point where I didn't get to do anything. I tried to negotiate with them but they were way too smart for me."

Once when Grant missed curfew by 15 minutes, Janet yanked the watch off his wrist and smashed it against a wall. "You don't bother to use this anyway," she said, "so why should you have it." Then she had it repaired and gave it to him on his next birthday. "That was my present," Grant said. "The same watch."

Grant didn't always have it so tough. For instance, he got his first car at 16. It was a Mercedes. "I hated it," he said. "A lot of teenagers would kill for a car like that, but I hated it. I was real sensitive about it. I was like, 'I don't like it. I don't want it. Why can't I have a normal car?'"

Grant, second from the right in the back row, and his South Lakes High team went to the Virginia state finals in his junior and senior years.

Grant didn't want to draw attention to himself. On the basketball court, he couldn't help it. He went wild his senior year. Grant averaged 30 points, 12 rebounds and 8 assists a game. He was Player of the Year a third straight time as he led South Lakes to the state finals again.

As Calvin was grocery shopping one day, a group of kids followed him from aisle to aisle. When they approached him, he was ready to sign autographs for them. Instead they asked, "Aren't you Grant Hill's dad?" Grant was no longer "Calvin Hill's son." Calvin had become "Grant Hill's dad." And Calvin was proud.

Grant competed against other future NBA stars in the
McDonald's High School Basketball Tournament.

On Top of the World

Grant's mailbox had been flooded with recruiting letters. It seemed that every major college in the country wanted him to play basketball. He had gotten all **A**s and **B**s through high school so he could go wherever he wanted.

Grant's mother wanted him to attend Georgetown University, which was just a few miles from home, and play basketball for coach John Thompson. Grant's father favored the mighty University of North Carolina and coach Dean Smith.

Everyone thought Grant would go to Georgetown. For a while, Grant thought so too. When he visited Georgetown, he met with coach John Thompson and an academic adviser. The advisor handed him a book. "Read this," she said. Grant read a page or so to himself and the adviser said, "No, I meant read it out loud." Grant read aloud as coach Thompson and the adviser sat quietly. The advisor stopped him after a few minutes and said, "OK, now tell me what you've read." Grant was offended by the test. They were checking to see if he could read. Grant knew he was a good student. "I walked out of the room knowing I wasn't going to Georgetown," he said.

Grant chose Duke University instead. "The day Grant picked Duke," said one of his friends, "was Grant's independence day." Grant liked the ivy-covered Duke campus in Durham, North Carolina, and he respected coach Mike Krzyzewski (SHAH-shef-ski). Other coaches told Grant that he would be a starter on their teams. They said that Grant would be the team's star. Coach K, as he is called, offered Grant a chance to compete. He said that Grant would have to earn a starting role.

When basketball practice began at Duke that fall, Grant was in awe. Here he was, playing against Christian Laettner, Antonio Lang, Bobby Hurley— athletes he had watched on TV. In his very first practice, Laettner dunked on him. From his dormitory room that night, Grant called his father. Grant told his dad that he didn't think he was good enough to play college basketball. His father reassured him. Grant called his dad often after that to hear his father's advice. As a nervous freshman, Grant wanted to hear his dad's PGAs.

Grant earned a starting role for the Blue Devils. He scored in double figures in Duke's first six games.

30

Grant was thrilled to play with Duke star Bobby Hurley.

But at times he seemed timid on the court. He didn't want to stand out. Coach Krzyzewski noticed. "Don't be afraid to be great," the coach told him.

Grant scored 19 points in each of the team's next three games. One night, Johnny Dawkins, who had played for Duke before joining the NBA, came to Cameron Indoor Stadium to see his old team play. After the game, Dawkins asked Grant who the best Blue Devil was. "Christian Laettner," Grant said. "No," Dawkins said. "You are." Grant was shocked.

The Blue Devils sailed through the regular season and easily qualified for the NCAA Tournament. The players wanted a spot in the Final Four. The Blue Devils easily won their first four tournament games to reach the semifinals. Against the University of Nevada at Las Vegas (UNLV) in the semifinals, Grant was assigned to guard Stacey Augmon. Some fans thought that matchup was a mismatch. UNLV had clobbered Duke by 30 points in the NCAA championship the year before and Augmon had been a big reason why UNLV won. But coach Krzyzewski believed that Grant was Duke's best defender even though he was a freshman.

Grant's parents were in the stands for the game. When Grant matched up against Augmon at center court, Janet said, "Whoa, our kid's in trouble." Calvin didn't speak. He didn't want to jinx his son. Part of Calvin's routine at every Duke game was to not speak unless necessary. Calvin was wearing the same outfit he always wore to Duke's games—a white turtleneck sweater, khaki pants, and a blue Duke basketball hat that he'd bought during Grant's recruiting trip. As always, Calvin held a cup full of ice in one hand and a box of peanut M&Ms in the other. At halftime, he would switch to chewing gum. He would give three pieces of gum to Antonio Lang's father, but none to anyone else. He did this every game. The routine never changed. "He's really superstitious," Grant says. "He's always been that way."

Maybe Calvin's ritual helped, maybe it didn't, as Grant played his best game of the year. He scored 11 points and frustrated Augmon with his defense. Augmon scored just six points, and Duke won by two.

Two nights later against Kansas, in front of 47,100 fans, including Grant's parents, Duke won its first national title. Grant set the tone of the game early when Bobby Hurley threw him an alley-oop pass. The pass was too high and too far from the basket but, somehow, Hill reached behind his head to catch the ball. He stayed airborne long enough to slam it. The Blue Devils won the game, 72–65.

Besides having an excellent basketball program, Duke University is a fine school. Grant's courses challenged him, but he studied and earned mostly As. He majored in history, minored in political science, and completed his degree in four years.

Grant's hustle makes him almost unstoppable.

Duke was ranked No. 1 in the nation as Grant's sophomore season began. Some teams crumble under that kind of pressure. Not the Blue Devils. They held the top spot from start to finish that year.

Midway through the season, point guard Bobby Hurley broke his foot. Coach Krzyzewski was asked what he was going to do. "I'm going to take my best athlete and make him the new point guard." And who was the team's best athlete? "That's easy," said Coach K. "Grant Hill." Grant directed the offense superbly. He led the team to five straight victories while Hurley's foot mended.

A player is shooting well if he makes half his shots. Grant did better than that. He shot an amazing 61 percent from the field as a sophomore. The problem was, he didn't shoot enough. He wanted to spread the ball around, making sure his teammates got their points too. "I look at him as a very humble athlete," Hurley said. "He's so unselfish it sometimes holds him back a little bit." Coach K agreed. "Grant is a reluctant superstar. He wants to be the best, but he doesn't want to separate himself from the team."

In the Atlantic Coast Conference final against North Carolina, Grant took eight shots. He made all of them. The Blue Devils won and Grant was named second team All-America that week.

Duke's dream of a second straight NCAA title was nearly shattered in the east regional final against Kentucky. Grant had 11 points, 10 rebounds, and 7 assists but the Blue Devils still trailed by two points with two seconds left in overtime. They needed a miracle. In the huddle, coach Krzyzewski said, "OK, here's how we win the game. Grant, you throw to Christian here and he'll take the shot to win." And that's just what happened. Grant threw a perfect football-style pass from under his basket to the other end where Laettner caught it at the top of the key. He turned, faked to his left, and put up a shot at the buzzer. It went in! Duke won 104–103. Janet and Calvin were jumping up and down with Duke fans in the temporary stands. Janet yelled, "I think these stands are going to collapse." Calvin yelled back, "Well if they collapse and I die, I'm going to die happy!"

Duke played the University of Michigan for the NCAA championship at the Metrodome in Minneapolis. Chris Webber and Jalen Rose, two players Grant had beaten as a 13-year-old in an AAU tournament, were among the team's respected "Fab Five" starters. Grant's team won again. Grant scored 18 points, grabbed 10 rebounds, and made 5 assists to lead the Blue Devils to a convincing 71–51 victory.

Janet and Calvin cheer for Grant and the other Blue Devils.

Grant and his teammates surround coach Mike Krzyzewski after Duke wins the national championship.

When Grant wasn't playing basketball, he liked other things about going to school at Duke. He played pool and Ping-Pong with friends at T.J. Hoops on Chapel Hill Road. He ate at McDonald's and browsed South Square and Northgate Malls. In the summer, he played on the Olympic development team. He also went to the White House where President Clinton named Calvin to the President's Council on Physical Fitness. Grant and his parents saw singer Aretha Franklin perform in the White House's Rose

Garden. They sat at the same table as Chelsea Clinton, the President's daughter, who was in junior high. Grant remembered how hard it was for him to grow up with a famous father. Grant figured Chelsea had some rough times too.

When Grant's junior season began, his life became frustrating. The trouble started in late January when he hurt his foot during practice. He played despite the pain. In a game against Wake Forest a month later, he landed awkwardly on the foot again just as two opponents fell on him. The other players got back up. Grant didn't. He had broken several bones in his foot and torn some ligaments. He missed the rest of the regular season. When Duke qualified for the NCAA Tournament again, Grant wanted to play. Coach Krzyzewski let him. But Grant's comeback didn't last long. Freshman sensation Jason Kidd and the University of California Golden Bears knocked out Duke in the second round. Grant had eight steals in the game but that wasn't enough. Duke's string of NCAA titles had ended.

Sportswriters named Grant to the All-America second team. They also named him the college defender of the year. Grant was more concerned about his foot and getting back to the Final Four. After spring exams, he had surgery. He wore a cast and spent the summer on crutches. Grant didn't play basketball again until a month before his senior season started.

After six months of being off his foot, he was pleased to find that it had mended well.

By Grant's senior season, the Duke team had changed. Christian Laettner and Bobby Hurley had graduated. A new cast of freshmen had joined the team. The experts predicted Duke to finish in the middle of the Atlantic Coast Conference. Grant thought of Coach K's message: "Don't be afraid to be great." Grant decided it was time.

Grant was 6-foot-8 but Coach K made him the team's point guard. Grant had tried just 19 three-point shots in his life, but during his senior season, he shot 100 and made 39—a good percentage from beyond the three-point circle. Passing and shooting were just part of what made Grant special that season. Most importantly, he became the team leader. He cheered his teammates in huddles. He put his arms around them during time-outs. He celebrated with them after a basket.

Freshman starter Jeff Capel had been struggling for three straight games when Grant gave him a pep talk before the team played the University of Virginia. Capel responded with a season-high 20 points in an easy victory. Grant scored 25 points, had 11 rebounds, made 5 assists, and blocked 4 shots, but he was more pleased with Capel's performance. "That's one of the reasons I chose to come here, because he was my favorite college player," Capel said. "I always wanted to have a chance to play with Grant."

Jeff Capel, left, and Cherokee Parks, center, look to Grant
for leadership during Duke's 1993–94 season.

Under Grant's leadership, the Blue Devils built a 21–3 record and were ranked No. 2 in the nation. "It's unbelievable the number of things Grant can do," said sophomore Chris Collins. "A lot of it goes unnoticed. He'll help out the guards defensively. He'll take a big charge. He'll get a rebound when we need one. Most guys have to score 30 points to have a great game. He can dominate by scoring 10."

But Grant could also score 30 points. When his team lost to rival North Carolina, Grant took it out on Clemson two nights later by scoring 33 points. Late in the game, he dived over a mob of players the way his father used to dive over the goal line. Grant suffered a black eye but he came up with the ball.

When Duke was playing Temple late in the season, the crowd at Cameron Indoor Stadium gave Grant a standing ovation when he came out for the pregame warmups. In a halftime ceremony, Duke officials retired Grant's jersey, No. 33. Janet and Calvin were filled with pride.

Duke won its first three games in the NCAA Tournament and advanced to the southeast regional final against Purdue. The Boilermakers were a powerful team with Glenn "Big Dog" Robinson, the nation's leading scorer. At practice the day before the game, Grant volunteered to guard Big Dog. Of course, Coach K would have told him to anyway. Shadowed by Grant all game, Robinson managed to make just 6 of 22 shots for a season-low 13 points. Duke won 69–60 to advance once again to the Final Four. After the game, Grant had kind words for Big Dog. "He didn't have a great game," Grant said, "but he had 37 great games up until then. So he was allowed to have a bad game."

In the Final Four at the Charlotte Coliseum in North Carolina, the Blue Devils beat the University of Florida in the semifinal game. But Duke's amazing run ended in the title game in a 76–72 loss to Arkansas.

Grant had led his team in nearly every statistical category. Grant was honored as a consensus All-America, but he wasn't concerned about individual awards. He was sad to see his college career end. "I can't believe how fast it went," he said. "But when I think about what we accomplished, I never would have thought in my wildest dreams it would have gone the way it did. It was amazing."

Coach Krzyzewski was also sad to see Grant leave. "Grant Hill is the best player I ever coached, period," he said.

Jason Kidd, left, who played for the Dallas Mavericks, and Grant share the 1994–95 Rookie of the Year honors.

Rookie of the Year

The Detroit Pistons were the "Bad Boys." They had won back-to-back NBA championships in 1989 and 1990 with a rough-and-tumble style of play. Isiah Thomas routinely drove down the lane with knees and elbows out. Dennis Rodman scratched and clawed for every rebound. Bill Laimbeer pummeled opponents.

By 1994 the Bad Boys' reign had ended. The team finished 20–62, last in the Central Division, 37 games back. By then, the last remaining player from the Bad Boys team was guard Joe Dumars, who was really a "Good Guy."

The Pistons needed to go in a new direction. They needed a new star. They needed Grant Hill.

Detroit would pick third in the 1994 NBA draft. Would Grant still be available? The Milwaukee Bucks had the first choice. Milwaukee officials made it clear they would draft Glenn "Big Dog" Robinson. But what would the Dallas Mavericks do with the second pick? The Mavericks said they would take Jason Kidd or Grant Hill. The Pistons would just have to wait.

As much as the Pistons wanted Grant, he wanted the Pistons. General manager Billy McKinney and coach Don Chaney had invited Grant and his father, along with Grant's agent, Lon Babby, to dinner a month before the draft. When Grant arrived at the restaurant, Joe Dumars was there waiting for him. "Joe didn't need to be there," Grant said. "That wasn't part of his job description, to wine and dine the draft choice."

But Dumars came, and he spent most of the evening listening intently to Calvin's old football stories. "That may not sound like much," said Grant, "but my dad can take 20 minutes to tell a five-minute story. I knew that by being there Joe was saying he wanted me in Detroit, and at that moment I knew I wanted to be in Detroit."

The Bucks opened the draft by taking Robinson as they had said they would. Then it was Dallas's turn. Coach Chaney was so nervous he had eaten four dozen oatmeal-raisin cookies. When the Mavericks said "Jason Kidd," Detroit general manager Billy McKinney jumped on the back of Pistons team president Tom Wilson. Tears of joy streamed down his face. Grant received a telephone call in his hotel room just an hour later. It was President Clinton.

"Congratulations, Grant," the president said. "I'm sure you'll make Detroit proud."

Grant flew to Detroit the next day for his first professional press conference. He held up a No. 33 Pistons jersey and said, "It still feels like a dream. Maybe I should pinch myself. Well, maybe I shouldn't or I might wake up."

Grant was asked about being a role model for children. "I think it's neat being a role model," he said. "There's a big void of role models in the NBA. Not that I'm going to fill that void. But hopefully there are some things I can do to make a difference."

The first thing Grant did, before he signed a contract with the Pistons or scored a single point, was to give $120,000 to the city of Detroit for a summer basketball program. Grant's program teaches academic and athletic skills to boys and girls, who range in age from 8 to 16. "Grant has put the children first," said a city official. When Grant and his parents went to a park to announce the gift, kids mobbed him. "Most of those NBA people just want to live the glamorous life and chill in their mansions," said a 13-year-old boy. "But he's taking time to be here with us and trying to help us."

The Pistons offered Grant a five-year contract for $17.5 million, a huge amount of money, but low for a No. 3 draft choice. "Let's take it," Grant said. "No, no, we've got to wait," said Babby. "They'll go much higher." "I just want to play," said Grant. "You will," said his agent. Grant signed his contract a week later. The contract was for eight years and $45 million. "It's not how much money you earn that's important," Grant said. "It's how much you save."

Grant's talent shocked his new teammates the first day of practice. "His first move was—boom!—just right by me," said Dumars. "That was the first move he made, just...boom! There's only one other guy I've seen do it like that...and...and I'm not even going to tell you who that was."

Dumars became Grant's tutor. He had Grant's locker placed next to his. In practice, pregame warmups, and timeouts, he made sure Grant stood next to him. "I feel like a sponge," said Grant. "I'm soaking up everything." Dumars admitted that the rookie superstar didn't have to listen to him. "But he does," Dumars said. "And he doesn't just hear, he listens."

Five seconds into his first exhibition game against the New Jersey Nets, Grant scored. Dumars hit him with a perfect alley-oop pass and—wham!—Grant slammed it. The rookie was off and flying.

NBA players and coaches couldn't stop talking about Grant. "He's an exciting, flamboyant player with great imagination," said Johnny Dawkins. "He's smooth as butter," said coach K.C. Jones. "We got the best player in college," said Dumars. "I see a lot of Michael Jordan in him," said coach Chaney.

Joe Dumars, left, talks to Grant about playing in the NBA.
The two teammates became good friends.

Some coaches compare Grant to Michael Jordan, left.

"The thing that lights me up is that he's a great defender," said coach Chaney. "Young players who come into the NBA have to be taught to play defense. Not Grant. He has those instincts already." A local newspaper columnist called Grant's $45 million contract, "a bargain for the Pistons."

By the time the regular season began, Grant had become even richer. He was making commercials. Among the products he was endorsing were FILA shoes, Schick razors, GMC trucks, and Spalding basketballs. He even had a line of athletic shoes named after him called "The Hill." For making the commercials, he earned $5 million a year. "You never think all this could happen to you," Grant said. "It's almost a dream."

50

When the season started, Grant delivered. On a cold, drizzly November night at The Palace in Auburn Hills, Michigan, he scored 20 points in his first game against the Los Angeles Lakers. Four games later, with Grant averaging 24 points to lead the team in scoring, the Pistons visited the Charlotte Hornets. Twice early in the game Grant drove fiercely down the lane and was fouled by center Alonzo Mourning. "C'mon, he's just a rookie!" Mourning yelled at the referee. "He isn't Michael Jordan!" Grant was having fun now. He knew he could play in the NBA. "Alonzo was getting frustrated," he said. "I like that."

In Detroit's eighth game, after a two-point victory at Denver the previous night, Grant showed the fans in Utah what he could do. On Detroit's first possession, Grant dribbled the ball up and down, up and down, at the perimeter. He was defended by Utah's quick forward David Benoit. Suddenly, Grant made a quick first step and blew by Benoit. He burst down the lane and flipped the ball into the basket. Benoit, getting there too late, fouled him. Grant shot a little smile to teammate Dumars. Dumars grinned back.

A week later Grant met Big Dog. Glenn Robinson's Milwaukee Bucks came to town and 21,454 fans filled The Palace to watch. Detroit double-teamed Robinson early in the game. During a timeout, Grant asked the coach to drop the double-team and let him cover Robinson. He had shut down Big Dog in the NCAA

Tournament. Grant figured he could do it again. He figured correctly. With Grant in his face, Robinson missed 12 of 14 shots, scored 9 points, and committed 6 turnovers. The Pistons won 113–108.

In a victory over the Golden State Warriors, Grant had 21 points, 8 rebounds, and 6 steals. Although Jordan had retired from the NBA and was playing minor league baseball, many people compared Grant to Jordan. "I don't think it's fair to Michael," Grant said. "The comparison is crazy. I hate it. It's foolish. I mean, he's the best player ever. I haven't done anything in this league, yet."

With Jordan out of the voting, Grant became the leading vote-getter for the All-Star Game. Grant had become the most popular player in the league. His popularity changed his life, sometimes for the worse. Fans mobbed him. He signed so many autographs that sometimes he thought his hand would fall off. He had to check into hotels with a fake name so fans wouldn't know where he was staying. And even then, he couldn't leave the room except for practices and games. When he was at home, he could only shop for groceries after midnight when the stores weren't full of people. During the day, he had to stay in his house, reading or watching TV or playing his video arcade games. One trip to a Detroit mall attracted such a swarm of fans that he couldn't get to the music store. He never tried again.

Delivering meals to those who need some help is one of the community service projects Grant does.

"I haven't bought any music since I moved here," he said. "I listen to the radio." Grant was enjoying his fame but it also was bothering him.

On the court, the Pistons struggled. They were out of the playoff race. With 10 games left in the season, Grant was asked about his chances of winning the NBA Rookie of the Year award. He had just tallied 25 points, 9 rebounds, 7 assists, and 5 steals against the Washington Bullets and their top rookie, Juwan

Howard. "It isn't even a goal of mine," he said. "If I had a vote, I'd vote for Juwan."

Then Grant thought about his father, about something his father had accomplished in 1969, his first year in the NFL. Grant thought about the Rookie of the Year trophy and he changed his mind about it. "Being Rookie of the Year is a goal of mine," he said a week later before a game at Dallas. "It's something I want to get." But while Grant was drawing comparisons to Jordan, Dallas point guard Jason Kidd was wowing fans with his fancy passing. Kidd reminded people of another superstar—Earvin "Magic" Johnson. It looked as if Kidd might win the rookie honor. That night against the Mavericks, Grant nearly got his first triple-double (double figures in three offensive categories) with 15 points, 9 rebounds, and 9 assists. "I want that award," Grant said.

Four nights later against the Boston Celtics, Grant set career highs with 33 points and 16 rebounds. Playing against the Orlando Magic at the end of the season, he got his first triple-double with 23 points, 11 rebounds, and 10 assists. He finished the season with a 19.9 scoring average and was 12th in the league in steals. Was his performance good enough to win the award? He would soon know.

Gentleman's Quarterly, a national magazine, put a picture of Grant on its cover with the words "Can Grant Hill Save Sports?" The article said that it was up to Grant to change the image of sports that had recently become a world of greed and egos. Grant was stunned. "Of all the things that have been said and written about me, this is the most absurd," said Grant. And then he joked, "Besides, I don't know anything about hockey and baseball." The magazine listed the 50 most influential people in sports. Michael Jordan was ranked 49th. David Stern, the commissioner of the NBA, was third. Grant was second, behind only Rupert Murdoch, owner of the Fox television network. "That doesn't make any sense," Grant said. "I'm ahead of the commissioner!"

Grant was more concerned about the Pistons. They had lost 8 of their last 10 games to finish last in the Central Division. It was the first time Grant had played on a losing team. But the reporters still named him Co-Rookie of the Year with Jason Kidd. Grant and Jason had become friends. They planned to spend their summer vacation together. Now they could show each other their trophies. "I don't mind sharing this award with Jason at all," Grant said. "It's an honor and it makes up a little bit for not being in the playoffs. This trophy was something I was shooting for. My father will have to make room for it because I'm giving it to him."

Grant's trophy sits today on his parents' mantel at their home in Virginia—right next to Calvin's NFL Rookie of the Year trophy.

Always a Winner

After his first NBA season, Grant spent his summer relaxing with Jason Kidd and appearing on television. He was on *The Tonight Show with Jay Leno* and even played a part on the TV show *Living Single*, in which he kissed performer Queen Latifah.

The Pistons fired coach Chaney during the off-season and hired Doug Collins to be their coach. Grant knew coach Collins. He had played with his son, Chris, at Duke. Doug Collins had often taken Grant and Chris out to dinner. When Grant was in a cast after his junior year, Doug Collins had sat and talked about basketball with him for hours. Grant knew coach Collins would expect the Pistons to play better than they had been. That's good, Grant thought, because he expected big things too.

When the season was about to begin, Joe Dumars took Grant aside and told him something that Grant would never forget. Joe said, "Grant, it's time for you to become a star. And do it right here, with me here. Don't wait for me to leave. I've had my time. It's your time. This is your team now." Grant heard him, and he took over.

From start to finish, Grant led his team in scoring, rebounding, assists, and steals. He was the only player in the NBA to do so. He became the 15th player in NBA history to lead his team in points, rebounds, and assists. He also led the league in triple-doubles with 10, two more than his friend Jason Kidd. With center Mark West, forward Otis Thorpe, and guards Joe Dumars and Allan Houston supporting him, Grant led the Pistons on a run toward the playoffs.

He also led all players in All-Star balloting again, even though Michael Jordan had returned to the league. "Just because more people voted for me than Michael doesn't necessarily mean I'm suddenly the more popular player," Grant said. "Apparently a lot of his fans didn't vote this time."

Grant played down the comparisons to Jordan, but he was thrilled to be an All-Star this time around. "Last year I was embarrassed," he said. "This year I feel like an All-Star. I feel like I belong."

Grant started the 1996 game at the AlamoDome in San Antonio, Texas, along with Jordan, Scottie Pippen, Shaquille O'Neal, and Penny Hardaway. Grant wasn't a bit nervous.

Grant blocks Shawn Kemp during the 1996 All-Star Game.

Orlando's Anfernee Hardaway, another young superstar, charges into Grant.

He scored eight points in the first six minutes of the game on a 19-foot jumper, a driving dunk, and two layups. He finished with 14 points as the Eastern Conference won easily.

The All-Star Game was fun but Grant had a bigger concern. He wanted the Pistons to make the playoffs. Basketball is a team game, but Grant thought it was his responsibility to get his team into the postseason. Down the stretch in close games, he simply took over. With the Pistons ahead by just three points in the fourth quarter at the Los Angeles Clippers, Grant scored eight straight points on a slashing layup, two free throws, a tip-in, and a bank shot. The Pistons won by four. A week later, when Detroit played Phoenix, Charles Barkley scored 45 points for the Suns. But Grant took over down the stretch, hitting three key baskets and finishing with 18 points, 17 rebounds, and 11 assists for another triple-double. The Pistons won by three. "I wanted this one," Barkley said. "I have to give Grant credit."

Some fans began to say that Grant could be the league's Most Valuable Player. "I'm not worthy of that award," Grant said. A week later, he was stretched out on the Pistons' training room table getting his ankle wrapped when a visitor told him he had been named the NBA Player of the Week. "Oh?" he said. "I am? That's the first time." Then he told a reporter that individual awards were not important to him.

The Pistons finished the season with a 46-36 record, which was good enough for the seventh spot in the playoffs. (The top eight teams in each conference qualify.) Grant was thrilled. The playoffs, the big games, this was what he wanted. Grant's joy vanished quickly. The mighty Orlando Magic swept the Pistons in three games to end Detroit's season.

"Comparing this year to last, I feel like I have aged 10 years," Grant said. "I welcome the leader's role. I enjoy it. And I've adjusted to being a celebrity. It's not fair that some star athletes can't go out and can't live a normal life. But it's not fair that you can play basketball and make a lot of money, either."

Grant's incredible basketball skills earned him a spot on the Dream Team, which represented the United States in the 1996 Olympics. "I'm confident in what I can do," he says. "My biggest fear is the fear of failure. I want to be the best there ever was. I want to go down in history. The only way to do that is to win.

"Don't take this the wrong way," he says, "but it's like Prince William. All his life he's taught to be king. That's what my parents did for me. They loved me and they shared with me all the good and bad about athletics and life. It's like they were preparing me. My secret ambition is to run for political office. I've always lived my life like one day I'd run for President of the United States."

Career Highlights

Duke University

Year	Games	Field Goals			Free Throws			Rebounds		Points	
		Made	Att*	% made	Made	Att*	% made	total	per game	total	per game
1990–91	36	160	310	51.6	81	133	60.9	183	5.1	402	11.2
1991–92	33	182	298	61.1	99	135	73.3	187	5.7	463	14.0
1992–93	26	185	320	57.8	94	126	74.6	166	6.4	468	18.0
1993–94	34	218	472	46.2	116	165	70.3	233	6.9	591	17.4
Totals	129	745	1,400	53.2	390	559	69.8	769	6.0	1,924	14.9

*Attempted

College highlights:

- Three-time All-America selection, including first-team pick in 1994
- Played on NCAA National Championship teams in 1991 and 1992
- Ranked ninth on Duke's all-time scoring list, sixth in assists, and fourth in steals
- His number (No. 33) was retired after he graduated.

Detroit Pistons (regular season)

Year	Games	Field Goals			Free Throws			Rebounds		Points	
		Made	Att*	% made	Made	Att*	% made	total	per game	total	per game
1994–95	70	508	1,064	47.7	374	511	73.2	445	6.4	1,394	19.9
1995–96	80	564	1,221	46.2	485	646	75.1	783	9.8	1,618	20.2
Totals	150	1,072	2,285	46.9	859	1,157	74.2	1,228	8.2	3,012	20.1

National Basketball Association highlights:

- Selected with the third pick in the NBA draft in 1994
- Chosen NBA Co-Rookie of the Year in 1995
- First NBA rookie in history to lead All-Star voting
- Fifteenth player in NBA history to lead team in points, rebounds, and assists in same season, in 1996
- Member of the U.S. men's basketball team, the "Dream Team," for the 1996 Olympic Games

ACKNOWLEDGMENTS

Photographs are reproduced with permission of: pp. 1, 50, 53, Allan Einstein; p. 2, SportsChrome East/West, Rich Kane; p. 6, Archive Photos/Blake Sell; p. 9, Detroit News photo by Clarence Tabb; pp. 12, 14, 17, 18, 40, 44, AP/Wide World Photos; p. 21, Photo by Steve Barrett; pp. 24 (both), 27, Courtesy of South Lakes High School "Freebird"; p. 28, McDonald's All-American High School Basketball Game; p. 31, Archive Photos/Gary Hershorn; p. 34, Archive Photos/Steve Jaffe; p. 36, ALL-SPORT USA/Damian Strohmeyer; p. 37, Archive Photos/Tom Russo; p. 43, Archive Photos/Tami Chappell; p. 49, Detroit News photo by Alan Lessig; pp. 56, 60, Archive Photos/John C. Hillery; p. 59, Archive Photos/Adrees Latir.

Front cover photograph by SportsChrome East/West, Rich Kane. Back cover photograph by Duane Belanger of The Detroit News.

Artwork by John Erste.

Index